I0737575

inner world

UNPLUG

SOFTCOVER RULED NOTEBOOK | 240 PAGES | ARCHIVAL PAPER

INSIGHTS
an imprint of
INSIGHT EDITIONS
www.insighteditions.com

Insight Editions, in association with Roots of Peace, will plant two trees for each tree used in the manufacturing of Insights journals.

INNER WORLD: UNPLUG
SOFTCOVER RULED NOTEBOOK
ISBN: 978-1-64722-220-8

9 781647 222208

MANUFACTURED IN CHINA

INNER WORLD

INSIGHTS
an imprint of
INSIGHT EDITIONS
www.insighteditions.com

MANUFACTURED IN CHINA
10 9 8 7 6 5 4 3 2 1

PROPERTY OF